STELLA ANDROMEDA

# CAT
## ASTROLOGY

### DECODE YOUR PET'S PERSONALITY
### WITH THE POWER OF THE ZODIAC

Hardie Grant

BOOKS

INTRODUCTION 5

DEDICATED TO MCVITIE AND WINTER COWLEY,
TWO CATS CLOSE TO MY HEART.

# INTRODUCTION

Just like us, every cat is born under an astrological sun sign which is determined by their date of birth. If you know the exact time and place of your cat's birth, you can have their astrological birth chart drawn up which yields even more information. However, even just knowing their sun sign will give you some insight into your cat's personality and character. This can in turn be helpful to your relationship and improve your understanding of how you might clash or chime with your puss.

From ancient mythology to folktales, the cat has been an important, often mystical and sometimes even scary companion to humans. The Egyptian cat goddess Bastet – both seductive and ferocious – was protector of the underworld. The first female child of Ra, she was linked to the powerful Egyptian goddess Isis and usually depicted in her company. We see something similar in the role played by the witch's black cat, said to be a shape-shifting familiar while the saying that a cat has nine lives comes from the old superstition that a witch could turn into a cat and back again eight times: but on the ninth time she would remain a cat forever. But if there is one thing that is crystal clear, whether we are talking about cartoon cats Felix and Tom, fashion designer Karl Lagerfeld's muse, Choupette, beloved children's book character Mog or even Dick Whittington's puss, it is how much we dearly love our cats with all their quirky ways.

# Cats choose us; we don't own them.

**LEWIS CARROLL,**
**AUTHOR OF *ALICE'S ADVENTURES IN WONDERLAND***

# FELIS CATUS DOMESTICUS

Cats were domesticated as far back as prehistoric times and greatly valued as working rodent catchers, as well as for their attractiveness and lively companionship. The first indication of this comes from 7,500 BC following the discovery of a cat skeleton resting near human remains in a Neolithic grave. Not only did the ancient Egyptians and Norse religions revere cats, they also domesticated them. These domestic cats were all descended from *Felis silvestris lybica* – the original wildcat. Yet, however domesticated a cat becomes, they retain an independence from their owners and often have secretive night lives, which may further explain why they have sometimes been so closely linked with black magic, making them also an object of superstitious fear.

# Time spent with a cat is never wasted.

**SIGMUND FREUD,
PHILOSOPHER AND FATHER OF PSYCHOANALYSIS**

# HOW CLEVER IS YOUR CAT?

Though their brains are small compared to ours, they're 90 per cent similar in structure. The part of a cat's brain responsible for processing information, the cerebral cortex, has about 300 million neurons compared to a dog's 160 million. They also have many more nerve cells in the visual area of the brain than we do, making their vision superb and enabling them to see in the dark and track and hunt their prey, including the smallest of mice.

What scientists have also discovered about cats is that they have longer-lasting memories than many other animals and learn by repeatedly doing something. They are also more impulsive, probably because they need to be able react so quickly, but also because they have the lithe, physical agility to be this way. The acute self-reliance of a cat can make them appear less socially inclined, only ever agreeing to be petted on their terms. Like the cat depicted by Rudyard Kipling in the *Just So Stories*, who said 'I am not a friend, and I am not a servant. I am the Cat who walks by himself.'

# Cats are smarter than dogs. You can't get eight cats to pull a sled through snow.

JEFF VALDEZ,
AMERICAN PRODUCER

# BIG CAT CONSTELLATION

The constellation of Leo is visible to the naked eye and consists of many bright stars, including *Regulus* or *Alpha Leonis*. The constellation commemorates the single-handed killing by Hercules of the Nemean lion that was terrorising the local people; a task that had been set by his cousin King Eurystheus as the first of Hercules' 12 Labours. The lion had been impervious to weapons and after Hercules' bare-handed victory, Zeus placed the lion in the sky.

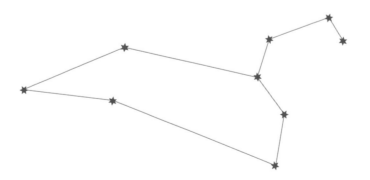

# FIRST CAT
# IN SPACE

French puss Félicette was one of 14 cats selected by
the French space mission and the first ever cat sent into
space. In 1963, she was chosen, thanks to her calm nature,
to orbit space so that scientists could record her neurological
reactions to this.

Félicette made the trip safely, returning to earth with
none of her nine lives spent, and, in 2019, her courage was
honoured when a statue crowdfunded by a Kickstarter
campaign to commemorate this brave cat was unveiled
at the International Space University in Strasbourg.

# A CAT MAY LOOK AT A KING

This ancient English proverb of unknown origin means
that whatever our place in society, we all have equal rights.
In ancient lore, commoners had to lower their gaze in the
presence of royalty.

Cats, as we know, are a law unto themselves and have
a particularly piercing, unwavering look: they lower their
gaze for no-one. And while looking anyone in the eye can be
interpreted as confrontational and perhaps a direct challenge
to their authority, it's in fact the sort of behaviour that says:
'we are equal'.

# A cat has absolute emotional honesty: human beings, for one reason or another, may hide their feelings, but a cat does not.

ERNEST HEMINGWAY,
AMERICAN WRITER

# LUCKY CATS

A black cat is associated with luck in many cultures, and in Japan all cats are said to be lucky, particularly the *maneki-neko*, the beckoning cat, and the rare, male tortoiseshell cat. Those cats born with extra toes are thought to be especially lucky, particularly for sailors at sea.

In Buddhism, from Siam (now Thailand) there's a belief that after death your soul is transferred to a Siamese (naturally) cat for safekeeping and that it is only when they die that you finally go to heaven. In medieval times, it was believed that cats ferried the spirits of the dead to hell, and in Norse mythology, the goddess Freya's chariot was pulled by two male cats who had been a gift from Thor.

Many of these ideas originate from a cat's night-time activities and independent nature. And you will already know that when your feline friend fixes you with an impenetrable stare it's hard not to believe that they too carry your secrets in their soul.

Introduction

# A CAT HAS NINE LIVES

**"For three he plays, for three he strays, for three he stays."**

This old proverb about a cat's nine lives plays on the fact that three is a sacred or magic number. We already know that in addition to its mystical powers, a cat has lightning-fast reflexes, along with great dexterity and a flexible body. This goes a long way to protecting them from those accidents (like falling from a tree) that could mortally damage a less-agile creature.

We tend to think of cats' lives as getting 'used up' and might refer to a battle-scarred cat which has just survived another scrape as using up yet another of their nine lives. But lucky as a cat is, they can't live forever and depending on their breed have a life expectancy of between 10 and 20 years, with most averaging around 15.

# BIRTH DATE

In an ideal world, you'd know the date, time and place of your cat's birth, but just having their birth date will tell you which of the 12 zodiac signs they are. If you are getting a new cat from a breeder, make a note to remember to ask for this information.

However, if you have given your cat a forever home from a rescue centre then you are unlikely to have this information. If this is the case, then you can take the date of their adoption into your life as the starting point of your relationship with them, which you will discover is just as meaningful.

And, of course, the more you learn about your cat's personality, along with the key characteristics of each of the 12 sun signs, then will soon find yourself quickly identifying which zodiac sign best sums up your cat.

Introduction

# Aries

## 21 MARCH–20 APRIL

Headstrong and occasionally wilful, this is a cat that leads by its whiskers and is independent to a fault. This is the cat that will carouse all night, lose its collar and get into fights, but will also be intensely loyal to you when you're around. Focus on that loyalty; reward it with time and attention when they demand it, and you will have a faithful feline for life.

Aries cats tend to act first and think afterwards and will often disappear into their own adventures, enjoying the hustle and bustle of the world beyond their fireplace and sometimes taking it a bit too far. If you have to call the fire brigade to rescue your cat from the top of the tallest tree because they're stuck, chances are you have an Aries cat. And that cat with a facial scar or torn ear? Aries, again, often diving head-first into trouble.

There's also a playful side to an Aries cat that endures long after they are no longer a kitten making them a lovely, responsive and fun pet to have around. In fact, being the most youthful of sun signs, an Aries cat retains its playful nature long into old age.

Your Arian cat will be the first to accept any new challenge, seeking always to maintain pole position, particularly if you have more than one puss sharing your home; although this cat will also be sociable enough to enjoy the company of its own gang.

FIRE SIGN

DEPICTED BY

# The Ram

RULED BY

# The planet Mars

LUCKY DAY

# Tuesday

WEAK SPOT

# The head (and over-exertion)

Aries ♈

# Temper that fire

An Aries cat can be prone to hyperactivity and burning the candle at both ends, so make sure you provide a soothing home environment to counteract their scatty cat ways. Regular hydration is important, and your cat may prefer cooler environments like a windowsill as a place to chill out.

# Working Aries cats

Many Aries cats are dedicated mousers and will hunt just for the pleasure of it, bringing home their booty as an unwelcome offering to you. Provide plenty of scratching posts to sharpen their claws, too, otherwise your furniture might suffer.

# Lucky colour

Your Aries cat's lucky colour is red which reflects their positive nature, so when it comes to choosing a collar or other feline accessories, from cat bowl to basket, choose red to reinforce that characteristic.

# Aries names

Fiery names for your moggy could include Brando or Tyson (meaning 'firebrand'), Drake (for a fire-breathing dragon), Kai (Scottish for 'fire') or Loki (a Norse trickster linked to fire). Enya, Elida, Tana and Fiamma are all names associated with fire, too.

# Aries cat match

If you are also a fire sign (Aries, Leo or Sagittarius) you will have a similar energy to your Aries cat, while their opposite sign is Libra.

# Aries breed

The Red Tabby, sometimes known as a ginger or marmalade cat, can be either short or long-haired. With its direct look and me-first attitude, this cat stands out in a crowd, marked by the Aries' colour red.

# Taurus

### 21 APRIL–20 MAY

The Taurus cat is one of the most straightforward of all felines, with a basic need for comfort and security. Less likely to be a keen mouser than some, the Taurus cat likes to take life easy and will happily just wait for you to provide what they want rather than go out to hunt for it. They're still as independent at heart as any other moggy but because Taurus likes to take the easy option, they prefer their food to arrive on a plate rather than having to chase it through the wild. And when it comes to food, they have a preference for gourmet but seldom refuse any, which can lead to problems of becoming overweight.

If you want a cat that will happily snuggle up with you, a Taurus cat is a good bet because they are more likely than some to enjoy being stroked and cuddled. In fact, this is a cat that will probably follow you around your home, settling close to wherever you are from dining room to bathtub. More communicative than some other sun signs, this is also a cat that will happily purr, meow and chirrup in response to your attention, happily stretching out to be caressed. But be warned, your Taurus cat will, if unhappy, also hiss or growl.

The Taurus cat doesn't much like much change and so will gravitate towards the same spot on the couch. Move the cushions or introduce a new item and it may well be treated with suspicion or even haughty disdain. That new dish you bought for your Taurus cat? It may take a while to be accepted.

EARTH SIGN

DEPICTED BY

# The Bull

RULED BY

# The planet Venus

Taurus

LUCKY DAY

# Friday

WEAK SPOT

# The neck, throat and sometimes the voice

# Pamper that earth

Long self-grooming sessions take up considerable time on the Taurus cat's not-very-busy daily agenda. They will happily accept a dirty tray, but this cat is a curious mix of earthiness and fastidiousness, and if their litter isn't regularly changed, they might well go and find somewhere else to do their business.

# Working Taurus cats

This is a cat that needs to be encouraged to work and is a bit '*meh*' when it comes to catching mice. The Taurus cat may be more easily persuaded towards domestic duties like keeping you company and your spot on the sofa warm for you.

# Lucky colour

Earthy greens and turquoise are your Taurus cat's lucky colours, so opt for a co-ordinating velvet collar, cat basket or other accessory within this colour range to play to their sun sign character.

## Taurus names

A green name like Parsley, Dill or Basil might suit your cat. Or Emerald, Jade or Moss. You might even consider a name like Bustopher Jones, the cat about town with a taste for fine food and smart clothes, from T S Eliot's *Old Possum's Book of Practical Cats*.

# Taurus cat match

Taurus relates well to the other earth signs Virgo
and Capricorn, while Libra's similar inclination
towards luxury may find a kindred soul. Fiery,
adventurous signs like Sagittarius may be a little
too rumbustious while a gentler water sign like
Pisces might work better.

# Taurus breed

Considered to be one of the more placid and sweet-natured breeds, the Manx cat has a double coat and no tail, making them look particularly rounded in the rump, and they love the daily brushing their coats need.

# Gemini

A mercurial nature might best sum up your Gemini cat's personality, unsurprising given that this is a sign ruled by Mercury, the god of communication. And this is a cat that will definitely communicate with you – with a purr, a meow or a tap of the paw to get your attention. This cat will keep you on your toes, full of energy and interest in their surroundings and, when it suits them, keen to be involved with whatever you do, following you around your home, interfering in your knitting or typing.

There's a duality to a sign depicted by the twins, however, and you could find yourself wondering if your puss has a dual personality, too, sometimes effusively interested in what you're up to and other times rather aloof. This, too, is normal for an air sign and Gemini is no exception, because this ability of being able to see things from two differing points of view gives them both enthusiasm and a cool rationality. Rudyard Kipling's Cat, the one that walked by himself from the *Just So Stories*, could easily have been a Gemini cat, flattering you when he chooses but essentially independent and, 'On moonlit nights he roams the woods or the roofs, walking by his wild lone self.'

Even into old age, this is a cat that stays curious and wants to be friends (on their terms, *natch*) with everyone, always keen to socialise and even party long past their bedtime, due to Gemini's innate fear of missing out! Given to mischief, this is also a cat that likes to take you by surprise and may even hide and reappear suddenly and unexpectedly from the top of the wardrobe to keep you on your toes.

AIR SIGN

DEPICTED BY

## The Twins

Gemini ♊

RULED BY

## The planet Mercury

LUCKY DAY

## Wednesday

WEAK SPOT

## The forelegs and shoulders

# Soothe that air

With all that wildness and duality, this is a cat that doesn't always find it easy to settle and can become hyperalert, which means some peaceful time-out is highly recommended. Make sure their bed is a secure, comfy and private space, although close enough to you so they don't feel left out.

# Working cat

Don't expect huge reliability from your Gemini cat as they will be far more interested in enviously watching birds in flight and trying to work out how they can take them down rather than in being a good mouser.

# Lucky colour

Sunny, citrus colours are lucky for Gemini, even those hues that drift into lime green; it's all about the zest of a colour for this cat. Choose from yellow and orange tones for a classy selection of collars or accessories, and even for their bedding.

# Gemini names

Mercury, Hermes or Ariel would be good name for your mercurial Gemini moggy, or Dinah, the cat from *Alice's Adventures in Wonderland* is an elegant literary reference. And if you had two Siamese cats, Si and Am were the twins from Disney's *Lady and the Tramp*.

# Gemini cat match

Air signs Libra and Aquarius find an affinity with Gemini, but too many airheads in a home might prove to be a bit much! Otherwise, as an earth sign like Capricorn or Taurus, or a gentle water sign like Cancer, you might find you create a better and more harmonious balance for yourself and your pet.

# Gemini breed

The striking blue eyes of the Seal Point Siamese breed suggests all the blue-sky airiness of Gemini and this sophisticated-looking breed is also renowned to be a 'talker' who loves to communicate, with a range of *meows* in a truly mercurial Gemini cat fashion.

# Cancer

## 21 JUNE–21 JULY

Is your cat a real homebody that loves nothing better than to snuggle up with you? Purring happily in your lap whenever they get a chance? Or bedding down in their favourite secret place for long, long naps? This sign is all about the home and family, and what makes it feel secure and loving is that strong and mutual commitment to family that is writ large in Cancer's personality.

Ruled by the Moon, which represents all things maternal, your cat's mothering instincts will be strong and may extend to you and yours as much as to her (or his) own feline family. They don't much like change, though, and can sometimes react badly to new places, new routines and new things.

The moon also affects the sea's tides and how they rise and fall and if you detect a certain moodiness in your pet's attitude, this might be why. This could show up as pickiness about food, which they generally love, or contrariness about a toy but it may not always be obvious because Cancer also has a tendency to hide their true emotions. Being this emotional also means your Cancer cat may have an almost uncanny empathy towards your mood, and indeed, of all the felines gifted with a sixth sense it's the Cancer cat that's most sensitive to your moods and feelings.

For all this sensitivity, however, this is a strong sign. Just like the crab with its soft centre, your cat's tender heart has a strong, protective shell into which they can retreat from time to time, in a quiet corner that they've made their own.

Cancer

WATER SIGN

DEPICTED BY

# The Crab

RULED BY

# The Moon

LUCKY DAY

# Monday

WEAK SPOT

# The belly and digestive system

# Soothe that water

For all their loving, communicative side, Cancer cats will need to retreat into the still waters of their emotions from time to time, taking time-out and perhaps hiding under the bed to get some peace if things get too rowdy or there's too much change.

Cancer ♋

# Working Cancer cat

If you ever need a feline babysitter, your Cancer cat is likely to be the one to happily allow a small child to (gently) play with them. They may also snuggle up close to a sleeping infant, mindful that they are a small person and alerting you if there's a problem.

# Lucky colour

The iridescent silvery blue-green colour of the sea is lucky for this water sign, especially when it gleams in the moonlight. Choose from this range of colour to enhance your cat's charms whether for their accessories, toys or favourite sleeping spot.

## Cancer names

Luna chimes with Cancer's moony influence, and even the name Moon itself. Other translations for moon include Selena, Diana, Deva, Aylin and Mahina. Or you could opt for something more watery or oceanic, like Marina or Maris, Neptune, Gill, Laguna, Rio, Orinoco or Thames.

 Cancer

## Cancer cat match

If you are also a water sign like Pisces or Scorpio, you'll easily understand your cat's inclinations, but it may be that your Cancer cat will commune more happily with a less emotional owner and actually prefer some of the warmer energy they will feel coming from an Aries or Leo owner.

## Cancer breed

Large, domesticated and not very vocal, the Maine Coon is a rugged looking cat that is devoted to its family. Historically associated with the sea, like the astrological crab, the cat hails from coastland Maine in the United States, reputedly arriving there on a Viking ship.

# Leo

The Leo cat doesn't just *think* he is king (or queen) of the jungle, he knows it and owns it. That pride of place on the sofa or sun-kissed garden seat? This is where you'll find your cat, always in the plum spot and without a second glance or a moment's consideration for a lesser mortal. This is an extrovert and exuberant character, always taking their time for a bit of preening and up for being noticed, admired and adored. If you don't cosset your Leo cat, they will let you know it because their cry for attention is more of an offended roar than a meow.

For all their regal ways, however, this is a puss with a purpose, and that purpose is their royal court and you. While they may treat you as their loyal subject, they are always loyal to you in return. You can rely on this commitment as part of a two-way process although you'll never be entirely sure exactly who's the owner of whom, and that's how your Leo cat will like it because having assumed as their birthright the role of the monarch, Leo isn't really a great team player.

You will notice that their kingdom extends beyond their immediate four walls, too, and they can be quite territorial about their patch so expect a few dust ups with the neighbouring cats if they come too close. For all their regal ways, however, a Leo cat is intensely loyal to those they consider their subjects, other household pets and humans alike.

$\Omega$

Leo

Leo

FIRE SIGN

DEPICTED BY

# The Lion

RULED BY

# The Sun

LUCKY DAY

# Sunday

WEAK SPOT

# The spine and the back in general

# Temper that fire

For this outgoing creature with its nose in
every saucer of cream, over-indulgence can
be a problem. Carousing all night also means
your partying puss has to recharge its batteries
somehow and some serious daytime downtime
may be the only answer.

# Working Leo cat

This is a creature that likes to show off, so there may be a theatrical role to be played in film or TV advertising, or at the very least on Instagram or YouTube. That cat that tinkles the ivories or licks its paws to order? That's probably a Leo working its audience with a professionalism that's impossible to fake.

# Lucky colour

Shades of yellow and orange like the regal gold rays of the sun are lucky for Leo whether for a grooming brush, decorative collar or scratching post. Gold reflects their sense of worth and while gold accessories may be a little *de trop* for other signs, not for Leo!

Leo

## Leo names

Anything with a royal twist like Rex or Regina is a good place to start, while names of monarchs from Arthur to Henry, Cleopatra to Victoria are also apt. Leo, Lenny, Leonora or Leonie work too, as well as Sunny, Solaris or Apollo.

# Leo cat match

If you're a fire sign, too, you'll instantly recognise your Leo cat's life-enhancing ploys, but there might be a bit of a clash of temperament between you. As an owner of this fiery feline, it might be useful to be a more temperate Libra, Virgo or Taurus and benefit from all that bossy energy.

Leo

## Leo breed

The Norwegian Forest cat or Wegie is known as a *scogcatt* in its native land and embodies many of this sun sign's characteristics. This is a big, brave cat that loves hunting and the long-haired varieties often look as if they have a Leo-like mane, needing regular grooming to look their best and which they'll also enjoy.

# Virgo

## 22 AUGUST–21 SEPTEMBER

If your cat strikes you as being rather particular about the food they eat, the bowl they eat from, the tree they'll climb or even the chair upon which they'll sit, chances are you're the proud owner of a Virgo cat. It's not so much that this is a fussy cat and it's not about being contrary either, it's about liking things *just so*. The upside of this is that you know where you are with this puss and can probably set your watch by the regularity with which they'll request their meal and turn in for the night. And letting you know what they want comes easily to a sign ruled by Mercury, the god of communication, with a wide range of purrs, meows and occasional yowls.

There's sometimes a touch of reserve, however, in the Virgo personality that can make them seem a little aloof and hold their ground, like the good earth sign they are. But a Virgo cat is a loyal pet that really won't give you cause to stress out. This is not a cat that will cause sleepless nights from going missing or staying out late. This is a moggy you can depend on. In fact, this is a cat that will sometimes appear to worry about *you*, tending to pick up on and reflect your mood. Like the other earth signs this is also a sensual cat, comfortable and confident in their physical prowess and agility, climbing trees and jumping with ease.

A Virgo cat will also reward your attention with loud purrs of appreciation, happy to soak up the stroking and winding themselves around your legs when they need to give and return some love. Then they're happy to retreat again to their own private world.

♍

Virgo

EARTH SIGN

DEPICTED BY

# The Corn Maiden

RULED BY

# The planet Mercury

LUCKY DAY

# Wednesday

WEAK SPOT

# The nervous system and gut, which are often interrelated

ℳ

Virgo

# Soothe that earth

Encourage your Virgo cat's playful side. It's
definitely there but sometimes needs a little help
to express itself, so make sure you encourage
your cat to have some fun and take some time-
out from the serious side of life, to enjoy a little
catnip and playtime with a favourite toy.

# Working Virgo cat

Attention to detail is what makes this cat a
fastidious mouser, and, as such, far less likely than
other astrological signs to leave a mess. They will
also keep you to a routine, letting you know when
it's time to get up which can make for a friendlier
alternative to the shrill of an alarm clock.

# Lucky colour

Blue and orange shades, from the palest tint to the strongest, most vibrant hue will bring luck to your cat and you can also use one hue to attractively enhance the other by contrasting combinations on any accessories, bedding or toys.

# Virgo names

Jennyanydots, one of *Old Possum's Practical Cats* shows all the signs of being a Virgo cat, organising the cockroaches into a 'troop of helpful boy scouts'! But the names Virgo or Virgil itself might suit this sign or, to match their enquiring mind, go for Aristotle, Plato, Hypatia or Simone after some of the great philosophers.

# Virgo cat match

If you, too, are a fastidious earth sign you may
well find this a harmonious pairing, but it may
suit you better to mix it up a bit; fire sign owners
like Leo or Aries can benefit from the calming,
organised style of a Virgo cat, while airy signs
like Gemini appreciate their grounding effect.

## Virgo breed

With its attractive dotty coat, the Ocicat is a rather
fastidious breed, but adaptable and friendly, with
a practical way of getting what it wants, much like
any Virgo. And if any cat can learn to open that
cupboard door to get its paws on the contents
(or tidy the shelves), the Ocicat can.

# Libra

## 22 SEPTEMBER–21 OCTOBER

This is a cat that likes balance and harmony, bringing a sense of this into the home, which makes them a delightful companion as they soothe the atmosphere with a delicate meow. And with a preference for a peaceful existence, a Libra cat is also diplomatic enough to compromise when it comes to maintaining the *status quo* and avoiding confrontation. In fact, a key characteristic is that of peacemaker and if you have several pets, you may notice how your Libran cat will be the one that decides life is too short for stress as they concede with grace over a shared toy.

Another key characteristic of your Libra cat is their charm. They will seek to please you and can be quite winsome in their efforts to get what they want. As well as being so charming, this is a cat prepared to weigh up both sides of any situation, so if you are waiting for a response to a new choice of food, say, this cat will take its time to decide. Snap decisions are not their forte. But once a decision has been made, they can be very definite about which they prefer and, with a Libra's taste for luxury, it's likely to be the gourmet choice.

Ruled by Venus, Libra is a pretty kitty who will spend time grooming and preening, well aware that their appearance gets them noticed. And attention is also something they love because this is a cat with a strongly social inclination, one that enjoys hanging out with you, happy to sit close by or on your lap while you work or watch television. Despite their general sociability, at heart with a Libran cat it's all about the one-to-one relationship they need to balance themselves, making a Libra cat an excellent choice as one of a pair.

Libra

AIR SIGN

DEPICTED BY

# The Scales

Libra

RULED BY

# The planet Venus

LUCKY DAY

# Friday

WEAK SPOT

# The kidneys and lower, sacral area of the back

Libra

# Balance that air

This air sign needs to be balanced by interaction with another and in the absence of other pets will regularly seek you out for some attention to achieve this. Your Libra cat will respond well to your voice and will love being talked or sung to. They may even enjoy the harmony of the music you listen to, too.

# Working Libra cat

When it comes to promoting harmony in a household, Libra's the cat for the job. Shy guests can be drawn out, conversation can flow (about them) and all social occasions improved by the socially minded and charming asset that is your feline friend.

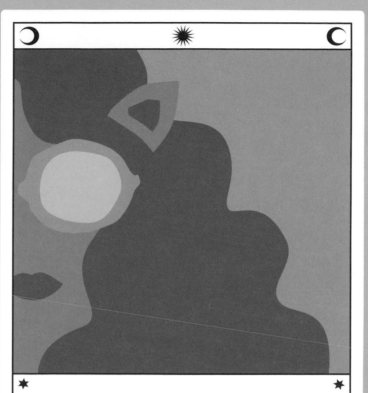

## Lucky colour

Pastel shades of blue, and irrespective of the shade, there's an airiness about these soft, muted colours that is lucky for Libra. Choose from across the blue spectrum to create a harmonious range of accessories for your stylish puss.

Libra

## Libra names

Charm being a key Libra trait, choose from some original charmers like Sinatra, Morrissey, Rhett or Paris. Equally, also Audrey, Grace, Hera or Lorelei. Perhaps even Rum Tum Tugger, from *Old Possum's Book of Practical Cats* because of his contrary nature, typical of many Libra cats.

# Libra cat match

If you're a Gemini or Aquarius, you'll find
harmony with a Libra cat. Water sign Cancer
also chimes, because you are equally committed
to a harmonious home, while earth sign
Capricorn provides some grounding ballast
for a Libra puss's airy take on life.

## Libra breed

There's a charm, elegance and discernment about a Burmese cat that fits the Libra profile, especially as its ancestors were thought to be the palace cats of Burma (now Myanmar). With a luxurious coat that needs plenty of attention this is also a cat that likes to set its own agenda.

SCO

# Scorpio

They may have rather a bad rep for being secretive and moody but look a little deeper and you'll find your Scorpio cat has many redeeming features, including a spiritual awareness that makes them almost psychic.

That inscrutable feline stare? He's got your number, but has also got your back, because loyalty to you is deep in the Scorpio DNA. It may not be immediately obvious, but, once committed to you, it's for life. So be aware that as far as your puss is concerned, that's how deep is their love. It's forever.

This cat is also very happy with a lot of solitude and, happily ensconced in the corner while you work or watch TV, you'll hardly know they're there. Scorpio's ability to hide in plain sight is one of their many mysteries but still waters run deep and that's how they like it, just on the edge of the action. And, however independently minded you believe your cat to be, when the moment is right those feelings emerge and you'll be showered with lots of moggy affection.

That affection can extend to all the neighbourhood cats, too, because another feature of Scorpio is an intense interest in recreation and creation, so if you don't want your roving Tom or Molly cat to endless carouse the night away producing lots of kittens, make sure they've visited the vet. That said, Scorpio cats tend to make very good parents so if you've got an interest in breeding a pedigree, this is a positive attribute.

♏

Scorpio

WATER SIGN

DEPICTED BY

# The Scorpion

RULED BY

# The planet Pluto

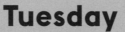

LUCKY DAY

# Tuesday

WEAK SPOT

# The reproductive organs, in both male and female

Scorpio

# Calm that water

All those intense feelings can occasionally weigh heavy on your Scorpio cat, so encourage some light-hearted play. And for a cat that tends to prefer dark corners and the mysteries of the night, encourage your moggy outdoors for daytime exploration, too.

## Working Scorpio cat

The strong silent type makes an excellent mouser, particularly at night as they instinctively prowl in the shadows. Happily, they're likely to be as secretive about their prey as anything else, so are less likely than other signs to present you with any grisly gifts after their hunting activities.

# Lucky colour

Deep dark reds, crimsons and burgundy colours
that almost touch on black resonate with the
passionate energy of Scorpio, enhancing their
luck in a collar or other accessories. Hiding away
in a womb-like bed is your cat's happy place, so
choose a deep red blanket to make it even cosier.

# Scorpio names

Macavity, the mystery cat from *Old Possum's Book of Practical Cats* is an archetypal Scorpio cat. Mystery, Enigma, Secret, Puzzler, Hush or Merlin are all Scorpio-like names while translations of the word 'secret' include Kasper, Rune, Amon or Hisoka.

# Scorpio cat match

This secretive type often needs the challenge of a more open sign, so if you are a straightforward Aries, or pragmatic Capricorn, you'll cope well with your Scorpio cat. Other signs that chime include fellow water sign Pisces, while lively Gemini brings a lighter touch to the relationship between cat and owner.

# Scorpio breed

Reputably one of the fastest breeds of cat, reflecting
the agile body and mind of Scorpio, the
Egyptian Mau is both playful and disdainful
by turn. A breed that doesn't mind water
either, they are as happy to explore a pond as
an aquarium or fishbowl, especially if there's
something to pounce on and catch.

SAGIT

# Sagittarius

## 22 NOVEMBER–21 DECEMBER

It's all about the journey for Sagittarius, and this is a cat full of wanderlust from the moment they look out of the window as a kitten, to chasing their dreams down the garden path and beyond. It's as if they fire off an arrow and race to see where it lands, and even in their dreams they might meow with the thrill of it all. Sagittarius has all the happy-go-lucky energy of Jupiter, its ruling planet, so this is a cat that radiates fun and adventure, making them a very endearing and rewarding pet.

The downside, however, is that they can wander far and wide and give you cause for concern. They won't get lost, but they easily lose track of time, staying out overnight and even disappearing for a day or two at a time on their explorations. No matter how independent they appear to be, they are actually glad to get back home, eat from their own bowl and recharge – ready for the next adventure.

This is an outgoing sign, where every stranger is just a friend they've not yet met, so expect your Sagittarius cat to be a friendly puss, happy to greet old friends and new. In fact, it's this friendliness that can sometimes get them into scrapes, because they don't always recognise antagonistic behaviour from another animal, who may be bigger and beefier than them. So be prepared for the occasional wounded warrior to limp home.

♐

Sagittarius

DEPICTED BY

# The Centaur

RULED BY

# The planet Jupiter

LUCKY DAY

# Thursday

WEAK SPOT

# The legs, particularly the hip joints

Sagittarius

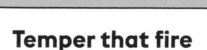

# Temper that fire

Whenever your cat is around, make a good fuss of her so that she knows for definite that the fire burns brightest on the home hearth and will always be happy to come home. Listen out for that excited chirrup as they bound in to tell you all about their latest fun times and make sure to respond and welcome them home.

## Working Sagittarius cat

Employed as a mouser on a travelling ship or train would be an ideal role for a Sagittarius cat, and even working as a ship's cat to travel further, would suit. One memorable name is Skimbleshanks, from *Old Possum's Book of Practical Cats*, who worked on the night mail train.

## Lucky colour

Glorious purple is lucky for Sagittarius, ranging from gentle violet to vibrant magenta and giving a lift to any collars, bedding or accessories. It's also a spiritual colour, which might chime with the occasionally seen, more philosophical side of your feline friend.

# Sagittarius names

Anything that implies exploration, adventure or travel, like Abeona and Adiona, goddess of outward and return journeys, respectively and also Hermes, Electra or Janus. Historical explorers Scott, Marco, Amelia or Gertrude, or purple colours like Amethyst, Violet to Periwinkle could work well, too.

# Sagittarius cat match

Sagittarius' friendly nature can be harmonious with many other signs, but if you are a fire sign too like Aries or Leo, you'll especially enjoy your pet's outgoing nature. Home-loving Cancer owners might find this cat a bit too adventurous, though, and Virgo doesn't always appreciate their waywardness.

# Sagittarius breed

There's something rather Sagittarian about the Aphrodite Giant breed. Originally from Cyprus they're all about the journey and adventure, whether that's to the end of the garden or further afield, but this is an active and engaging cat that also loves its home.

CAPRI

CORN

# Capricorn

There's a cool capability about Capricorn that you may spot in your cat, something in the way they like to arrange where they sleep, eat or generally hang out. Did you really just catch your puss reorganising its litter tray into a tidy heap? With this cat it's entirely possible.

There's an in-built patience, too, about this cat, who shows little anxiety about what's going to happen next or when. They trust that you'll feed them on time and, if not, their gentle nudge will remind you.

Down to earth but no pushover, this is a cat that knows the value of just putting one foot in front of the other to achieve their goal, just like the sure-footed mountain goat that represents this sign. Whether this is climbing that tree, negotiating the garden or nudging you into play, Capricorn expects their patience to be rewarded. Self-contained almost to a fault, their demands are few, but they do expect their loyalty – another Capricorn trait – to be returned.

Don't underestimate your Capricorn cat's capacity for playfulness either. When the mood takes them, Capricorn can be a skittish kitten, shadow boxing dust motes in a beam of sunlight, pouncing with glee on that toy mouse, headbutting you to make you smile. They're a social and communicative sort, happy to listen with their head on one side before responding with a thoughtful meow, yowl or purr, whichever is appropriate.

DEPICTED BY

# The Mountain Goat

RULED BY

# The planet Saturn

LUCKY DAY

# Saturday

WEAK SPOT

# The joints and a susceptibility to arthritis

Capricorn ♑

# Pamper that earth

Given how undemanding this zodiac sign is, make sure you remember to give them the love and attention they deserve as they won't always ask for it, being cautious about interrupting your day. Lots of conversation, gentle stroking and lap time will be greatly welcomed.

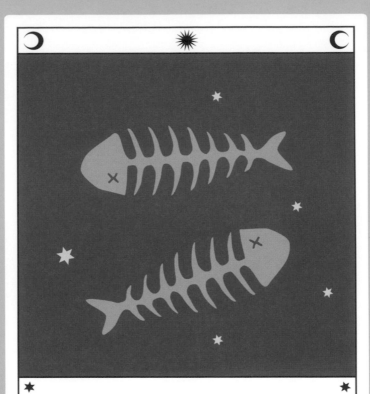

# Working Capricorn cat

This is a cat that takes work seriously and will diligently apply the rules of the chase, the catch and the disposal. Neat and tidy too, this cat won't be showing off its kill, but will discretely tidy away any messy carcass. So, if you're squeamish about being gifted entrails, this is definitely the cat for you.

# Lucky colour

Those earthy tones of brown and green that resonate with their grounded nature are lucky for your Capricorn cat. These tones can be as muddy or as vibrant as nature intended, to enhance your cat's character, from collars to a favourite rug.

# Capricorn names

No surprises that Capability Brown was a gardener, loving the earth and patiently waiting for the plants to grow. Other gardeners include Gertrude Jekyll, Sir Geoffrey Jellicoe and Vita Sackville West. Or to reflect the goat, Billy, Pan or Schwanli and Baerli from the story of *Heidi*.

Capricorn ♑

146

## Capricorn cat match

This calmly loving earth sign is a good match
for a flighty air sign owner like Libra or Aquarius,
although fellow earth signs Virgo and Taurus
are immediately compatible, and sensitive water
signs like Pisces and Cancer find Capricorn pets
gently reassuring.

# Capricorn breed

Renowned for being the highest climbers, like the Capricorn goat, the Abyssinian cat is also graceful, steadfast and sure-footed. Inquisitive and intelligent, they will work hard to reward you with playful attention.

# Aquarius

## 21 JANUARY–19 FEBRUARY

Freedom lies at the core of an Aquarius cat's soul. Freedom of spirit, freedom to roam, freedom of heart, this is an independently-minded creature who is all about the bigger picture. She loves you, sure, but she also loves the whole world, so if you see your puss being super-friendly to the neighbours, don't worry, it's just the way she is. Making connections between you and other family and friends also interests this cat, and you may sometimes feel as if they are sizing up the situation, looking from one to another of you as you talk. Even interjecting the occasional quizzical meow.

Because an Aquarius trait is basically to love the whole world and everything in it, you could be forgiven for thinking this is a cat that doesn't care that much for you, but that wouldn't be true. Their commitment comes with no strings attached and while their undemanding nature can look emotionally detached, the truth is, they love you unconditionally, even if they just don't show it.

The other thing Aquarius loves is puzzles, so you will likely find that this is a moggy with a very active mind, always investigating how something works. From that clockwork toy to the television, your curious cat may watch and try to interact with what's fascinating them in ways that may surprise you, finding innovative new uses for that TV remote. And if you find your cat investigating all sorts of surprising things around the house, from the laundry basket to your computer mouse, well that's just par for the course for this quirky feline.

Aquarius ≈≈

AIR SIGN

DEPICTED BY

# The Water Carrier

RULED BY

# The planet Uranus

LUCKY DAY

# Wednesday

WEAK SPOT

# The circulation, blood and lymphatic system

# Temper that air

When it comes to cuddling your cat, you may have to take your cue from them and drop what you're doing for that special moment, on their terms. This is a cat that needs to be encouraged to express their love through light-hearted interactions, gentle play and conversation rather than rumbustious games.

# Working Aquarius cat

This is a creature that wants to strategise its working moves, thinking things through before pouncing. If your cat sits for long hours watching the birds through a window, this is not idle time-wasting, but working out the best way to tackle the problem due to their lack of wings.

# Lucky colour

Sky-blue, the colour of the air above us, is lucky for your Aquarius cat. It's all about the shades of light, rather than dark blue that will enhance your pet's collar and accessories, but within that range there's plenty of choice for a stylish moggy.

## Aquarius names

Derivations of Charles, Carl or Carlos mean 'free man', as does Francisco, Francesca or Frankie, while Liberty is all about freedom and Lysander/Lysandra means 'liberator': all suitable names for this free-spirited cat.

# Aquarius cat match

This lovely airy energy makes a great companion pet for the earthier of us, Taurus or Virgo, while Libra and Gemini share similar traits, and fire sign owners Aries and Leo bring a little warmth to the relationship between owner and cat.

# Aquarius breed

The Russian Blue cat has something of an Aquarian air. Although once known as the Archangel cat, increasing its celestial status, this breed is slightly aloof but very much interested in showering their human family with love.

# Pisces

Empathic, almost to the point of being analytical, the Pisces cat is the classic psychic puss who seems to be able to sense your every mood, from the moment you walk through the door. If you need time alone, they'll steer clear but when they sense you need a reassuring snuggle or to be persuaded into some fun, there they will be, by your side. There's nothing sweeter than when this affectionate creature snuggles up, sharing your sorrow or your joy.

The downside of a cat with all its emotions washing about is that these can sometimes get a bit overblown, so this is the cat that might need your reassurance during a thunderstorm or a firework display, as they'll inevitably imagine the worst! Your proximity is usually enough to soothe them although for the more timid of pets, a snug dark corner under the bed or the cosy and safe inside a cupboard might be required until all the excitement has passed.

Surprisingly enough, a Pisces cat is one of the least demanding because they have such an active internal life, full of imagination, they are very seldom bored. If you have another household pet, they are companionable souls and tend to get along with other cats (and dogs) well.

They love to play, too, and you will be kept amused for hours by a Pisces kitty's imaginative antics. Even in their dreams they're probably still chasing imaginary mice and butterflies, making their snoozing whiskers twitch and their tail flick.

WATER SIGN

DEPICTED BY

# Two Fish

RULED BY

# The planet Neptune

LUCKY DAY

# Friday

WEAK SPOT

# The feet, so may be liable to foot problems

# Calm that water

Still waters run deep with Pisces and you may
not always know what's going on inside that
head, although twitchy dreams can also be happy
ones. But sometimes this sensitive kitty may just
need the reassurance of your company to get
them through a stormy patch, so be sure to stroke
and comfort if needed.

Pisces

# Working Pisces cat

There's something slightly theatrical about a Pisces cat that might make training them for advertising, photography or film work a good choice – think of the success of *Keanu* (the movie) that used seven trained tabby cats, Binx in *Hocus Pocus*, and the villain Blofeld's cat in the James Bond movies.

168

# Lucky colour

Turquoise, the blue/green of a sparkling sea, lake or river, is Pisces' lucky colour, hardly surprising given this water sign is depicted by fish and ruled by Neptune. Choose elegant shades to enhance your cat's charm in a collar, bed or rug.

# Pisces names

Pisces itself, or perhaps Neptune? Other names
resonating with the element of water include
Marina, Nerida, Circe, Darya or Maya for a
female, Brook, Kai or Misty are unisex, while
Murray, Dylan, Jordan, Irving or Lachlan might
work for a Pisces tom cat.

# Pisces cat match

While other water signs appreciate the dreaminess of Pisces, a more robust earth sign like Capricorn or fire sign like Sagittarius might bring a bit of balance to the relationship between cat and owner. Gemini and Libra also work well, although their airiness might occasionally ruffle Pisces' fur.

## Pisces Breed

Nimble, intelligent and with an affinity to water, the beautiful coat of the Bengal tabby marks out a breed that takes its name from the Asian leopard. Alert and easily bored, this is also a cat that genuinely enjoys human company and will seek you out as its favourite friend.

# About the Author

Stella Andromeda has been studying astrology for over 30 years, believing that a knowledge of the constellations of the skies and their potential for psychological interpretation can be a useful tool. This extension of her study into book form makes modern insights about the ancient wisdom of the stars easily accessible, sharing her passionate belief that reflection and self-knowledge only empowers us in life. With her sun in Taurus, Aquarius ascendant and moon in Cancer, she utilises earth, air and water to inspire her own astrological journey.

# Acknowledgements

Particular thanks are due to Kate Pollard, Publishing Director at Hardie Grant, for her Taurean passion for beautiful books and for commissioning this series. And to editor Eila Purvis, for all her hard work and attention to detail. While the illustrations and design talent of Evi O Studio have produced small works of art. With such a star-studded team, these books can only shine and for that, my thanks.

Published in 2021 by Hardie Grant Books,
an imprint of Hardie Grant Publishing

Hardie Grant Books (London)
5th & 6th Floors
52–54 Southwark Street
London SE1 1UN

Hardie Grant Books (Melbourne)
Building 1, 658 Church Street
Richmond, Victoria 3121

hardiegrantbooks.com

British Library Cataloguing-in-Publication Data. A catalogue record for this
book is available from the British Library.

Cat Astrology
ISBN: 978-1-78488-387-4

10 9 8 7 6 5 4 3

Publisher: Kajal Mistry
Editor: Eila Purvis
Design and Illustrations: Evi-O.Studio
Copyeditor: Susan Clark
Production Controller: Katie Jarvis

Colour reproduction by p2d
Printed and bound in China by Leo Paper Products Ltd.